YOUR KNOWLEDGE HAS VALUE

- We will publish your bachelor's and master's thesis, essays and papers

- Your own eBook and book - sold worldwide in all relevant shops

- Earn money with each sale

Upload your text at www.GRIN.com and publish for free

Anna Uhlhorn

Henry James "Washington Square". Eine Analyse

GRIN Verlag

Bibliografische Information der Deutschen Nationalbibliothek:

Die Deutsche Bibliothek verzeichnet diese Publikation in der Deutschen National-
bibliografie; detaillierte bibliografische Daten sind im Internet über http://dnb.d-
nb.de/ abrufbar.

Imprint:

Copyright © 2012 GRIN Verlag GmbH
Druck und Bindung: Books on Demand GmbH, Norderstedt Germany
ISBN: 978-3-656-55538-4

This book at GRIN:

http://www.grin.com/en/e-book/265838/henry-james-washington-square-eine-
analyse

GRIN - Your knowledge has value

Der GRIN Verlag publiziert seit 1998 wissenschaftliche Arbeiten von Studenten, Hochschullehrern und anderen Akademikern als eBook und gedrucktes Buch. Die Verlagswebsite www.grin.com ist die ideale Plattform zur Veröffentlichung von Hausarbeiten, Abschlussarbeiten, wissenschaftlichen Aufsätzen, Dissertationen und Fachbüchern.

Visit us on the internet:

http://www.grin.com/

http://www.facebook.com/grincom

http://www.twitter.com/grin_com

Response Paper on Henry James' *Washington Square*

Handed in by Anna Severin

11/22/2011

The novel "Washington Square", written by Henry James in 1880 takes place during the
1840s in New York, in the neighborhood of Washington Square. The story can be
summarized and sub-divided into different actions of drama: Firstly, the reader is
provided with the family background of the main characters. The author starts off with a
detailed portray of Austin Sloper, a distinguished and well-known physician and he is
about 50 years old when the story takes place. His wife Catherine first gave birth to a
son who died few years after his birth. Later, Catherine gave birth to a girl who is
named after her, but she died in childbed. Catherine, around which the storyline centers,
can be characterized as the heroine of the novel. She is about twenty-two years old
when the drama is set. From the day of her birth and throughout her whole life, Dr
Sloper sees his only child as a "disappointment" (p.7) for her not being a boy, not being
as beautiful as her mother or as clever as her father, which can be identified as the
source of the main conflict between them. Moreover, Dr. Sloper has two sisters,
Lavinia Penniman, once married to an impoverished clergyman, now widowed and
living with the Slopers, and Elizabeth Almond, who is married to a successful merchant
and the favorite of her brother for having succeeded in life and establishing a wealthy
lifestyle. On the contrary, Aunt Lavinia moves in with her brother when Catherine is a
few years old and of whom Dr Sloper thinks to be a good surrogate mother for
Catherine, but in fact "Mrs. Penniman had not made a clever woman of her" (p. 12).
Further, Catherine is characterized by her own father as being a "commonplace child"
(p.12), as limited in mind, as "dull, plain [...], quiet" (p.14), and in addition, as "both
ugly and overdressed" (p. 14), which are harsh words when talking about his own
daughter, but he does not hide his opinion from her. Also, Catherine is very afraid of her
father and "her deepest desire was to please him, and her conception of happiness was
to know that she had succeeded in pleasing him" (p. 12), what barely happened as one
can manifest in the ongoing storyline.

At the age of twenty-one, Catherine even worsens their conflict by downgrading her father's opinion of her, when she starts to overdress herself, especially when she is wearing a "red satin gown trimmed with gold fringe" (p. 15) to her aunts party, which made her look "like a woman of thirty" (p.15). Simultaneously, the commercial development in New York is at its highest and the "tide of fashion began to set steadily northward", where Dr Sloper is moving his household too. His aim is to get away from traffic and to settle in "a handsome, modern, wide-fronted house, with a big balcony before the drawing –room windows […], marble steps ascending to a portal" (p. 15f.), which are according to the author Henry James, to "embody the last results of architectural science". Washington Square stands for the growing American nation and the running up of New York, where its residents build huge mansions and from where they could overlook the greater surroundings and escape the overpopulation in lower Manhattan. This place was reserved for the wealthy citizens like Dr Sloper and his family. Another remarkable aspect of this story is that the whole action seems to take place in some kind of bubble, distracted from reality and all its political and social happenings at this time. For instance, Dr Sloper and Catherine as well as all other characters in this novel seem to live a peaceful live, unaffected by the civil war which erupted at this time.

To return to the story, at this aforesaid party of her aunt Elizabeth, Catherine makes the acquaintance of Morris Townsend, a handsome and good-looking young man, who is very interested in Catherine as he later confesses to her aunt Penniman. Morris Townsend has been away from New York travelling to all important places and has spent all his fortune. In fact, the reader also learns that he is living off his widowed sister Mrs. Montgomery, as he refuses to carry on a job, which portrays him to be very selfish. His intention is to marry Catherine after some time of courting her, which arises another conflict between father and daughter, as Dr Sloper does not like Morris Townsend to marry his daughter, for he believes him to be hypocrite who is just after his daughter's fortune. This fact imposes a strong inner struggle in Catherine, as her personal desire clashes with the parental love. Catherine, for whom the greatest wish is to please her father and to make him proud of her, is certain that Morris loves her and agrees to marry him. The fact is, Austin Sloper was never able to love his daughter as he always regarded her as a disappointment and never thought of her to get married, which results in her being even more certain in marrying the first man who confesses his love to her. Moreover, Catherine's lack of self-value, which is to be traced back to her father not valuing her as a obedient and loving daughter, contributes to her disobeying her father's wish to not see Morris again. The striking point about this conflict is that at the time the story takes place, women had only limited rights and a marriage was often a business deal rather than out of love. Men like Morris Townsend were expected to provide for their future wife and family. After marriage, the husband was in charge of all household money, a fact that Austin Sloper fears when Morris Townsend marries his daughter and therefore all her fortune left by her mother, a fact he tries to make clear to her, without success. However, Dr Sloper's true intentions to impede on his daughter's marriage do not clearly come true throughout the storyline. Over all, he tries to save his daughter's fortune by not marrying an impoverished and indolent man, which concludes that he, after all, has feelings for his daughter and does not want her to end in misery.

On the contrary, he himself once married a wealthy woman, Catherine's mother, but still cannot believe someone would marry his daughter for love. Evidently, Dr Sloper lacks family feeling, like pride, love or caring for each other. Throughout the novel, he is pictured as being cold and emotionally detached from his daughter and as being cruel for separating Catherine and her lover, both physically and emotionally when taking her to Europe. This contrast between warm and cold, good and evil is pictured particularly in chapter eleven, when Catherine goes to see her father in his study in order to inform him about her engagement with Morris Townsend. First of all, this change of setting symbolizes the character's emotional condition. Catherine never entered her father's study without knocking at his door, as it functions as a retreat for him. During her conversation with her father, she permanently looks at the fireplace which was "much warmer" (p.54) than her father's eyes or his saying. This scene presents the negative conflict and the lack of a functioning filial-paternal relationship. The imagery of 'coldness' reoccurs again at the end of the novel, when Dr Sloper dies of a cold he got visiting a patient, however he himself diagnosed "congestion of the lungs" (p. 163), he still cannot admit that he did his daughter wrong in putting a ban on her marriage so she would become an old maid. He "had never been wrong in his life, and he was not wrong now" (p. 163), that is how he characterizes himself at last. After his death, Catherine and her Aunt Penniman continue to live in Washington Square and over the years,

Catherine has not heard again from Morris Townsend. Both are presented as more independent and free of Dr Sloper's control. Only once, her aunt informs her that Mr. Townsend is back in New York, which causes Catherine to collapse and burst into tears. The reoccurrence of her former lover represents once again her former conflict with her father and reminds her of their distorted relationship and her lost love. However, when Catherine is confronted with Morris' presence, she detects that all her feelings for him are dead. When he has left, Catherine finally picks up her needlework and seats herself" for life, as is were" (p.174), which again depicts her conflict with her father and her 'resigning' with her own happiness. Finally, she has found her freedom, but she still is alone, like she has been when her father was still alive.